Title:

Quantum Paths: Building Quantum Solutions with Qiskit

Table of Contents:

7. **Chapter 7: Interpreting the Quantum Melody**

   o **Analyzing Quantum Circuit Results**

   o **Analogy:** Reading the Audience – Interpreting the Outcomes of Quantum Computations

   o **Concepts Covered:** Measurement Results, Probability Distributions, Error Analysis

8. **Chapter 8: Tuning the Quantum Orchestra**

   o **Optimizing and Improving Quantum Circuits**

   o **Analogy:** Fine-Tuning the Instruments – Optimizing Quantum Solutions

   o **Concepts Covered:** Circuit Optimization, Error Mitigation, Advanced Techniques

9. **Chapter 9: The Quantum Encore**

   o **Deploying and Sharing Quantum Solutions**

   o **Analogy:** The Curtain Call – Sharing Your Quantum Masterpiece with the World

   o **Concepts Covered:** Deploying Solutions, Sharing with the Community, Open Source Contributions

10. **Chapter 10: The Future of Quantum Symphony**

   o **Looking Ahead in Quantum Computing**

   o **Analogy:** The Next Composition – The Future of Quantum Solutions

   o **Concepts Covered:** Emerging Trends, Quantum Supremacy, Future of Qiskit

Chapter 1: Introduction to Quantum Computing

Song of the Quantum Realm: Understanding Qubits and Superposition

In the vast expanse of the quantum realm, the fundamental building blocks are not classical bits but qubits. Understanding these qubits is crucial to grasping the essence of quantum computing.

Analogy: The Quantum Orchestra – How Qubits Play Together

Imagine a grand orchestra preparing for a symphony. In a classical orchestra, each musician plays a specific note, and the combination of these notes creates harmonious music. However, in a quantum orchestra, the musicians (qubits) have unique abilities that classical musicians do not. They can play multiple notes simultaneously, and the combination of these notes isn't fixed until the conductor signals the end of the piece.

1. **Qubits as Musicians:**

    o **Classical Bits vs. Qubits:** In classical computing, bits can be in one of two states: 0 or 1. In our orchestra analogy, this would mean each musician could only play a single note, either C or G.

    o **Qubits:** In contrast, qubits can exist in a superposition of states. This means a qubit can play a blend of C and G simultaneously until measured. This unique capability allows quantum computers to perform complex calculations more efficiently.

2. **Superposition – The Melody of Possibilities:**

    o **Superposition:** Just as a musician in the quantum orchestra can play multiple notes at once, a qubit can exist in a superposition of 0 and 1. This property is what gives quantum computers their parallelism and potential for exponential speedup in certain tasks.

    o **Mathematical Representation:** Mathematically, if we represent the state 0 as $|0\rangle$ and the state 1 as $|1\rangle$, a qubit in superposition can be written as $|\psi\rangle = \alpha|0\rangle + \beta|1\rangle$, where α and β are complex numbers representing the probability amplitudes.

3. **Entanglement – Harmonizing Qubits:**

- **Entanglement:** In a classical orchestra, musicians play their parts independently. In the quantum orchestra, however, musicians can become entangled. When qubits are entangled, the state of one qubit is directly related to the state of another, no matter the distance between them.

- **Example:** If two qubits are entangled, measuring one qubit will instantly determine the state of the other. This phenomenon is akin to two musicians playing perfectly synchronized notes, even when separated by great distances.

4. **Measurement – Collapsing the Symphony:**

   - **Measurement in Quantum Mechanics:** When we measure a qubit, the superposition collapses to a definite state, either 0 or 1. This is similar to the conductor bringing the orchestra to a halt, at which point each musician's note becomes fixed and audible.

   - **Implications for Computing:** Measurement is a critical step in quantum algorithms, determining the final outcome of computations.

Concepts Covered: Qubits, Superposition, Entanglement, Measurement

1. **Qubits:**

   - **Definition:** The fundamental unit of quantum information, analogous to a classical bit but with quantum properties.

   - **Physical Realizations:** Qubits can be realized using various physical systems such as trapped ions, superconducting circuits, and quantum dots.

2. **Superposition:**

   - **Explanation:** The ability of a qubit to exist in multiple states simultaneously. This property enables quantum computers to explore many possible solutions at once.

   - **Visual Representation:** Superposition can be visualized using the Bloch sphere, where any point on the sphere represents a possible state of the qubit.

3. **Entanglement:**

- o **Explanation:** A quantum phenomenon where the states of two or more qubits become linked, such that the state of one qubit is dependent on the state of another.

- o **Applications:** Entanglement is a key resource in quantum computing, used in algorithms like quantum teleportation and quantum key distribution.

4. **Measurement:**

- o **Explanation:** The process of observing the state of a qubit, causing its superposition to collapse to a definite state.

- o **Outcome:** Measurement outcomes are probabilistic, governed by the probability amplitudes of the qubit's state.

In-Depth Exploration

In this chapter, we will dive deeper into each of these concepts, exploring their mathematical foundations, physical implementations, and roles in quantum computing algorithms. Through the analogy of the quantum orchestra, we will uncover the beauty and complexity of the quantum world, setting the stage for more advanced topics in subsequent chapters.

Detailed Breakdown

1. **Qubits – The Quantum Musicians:**

- o **Physical Representations:** Discuss different ways qubits can be implemented (e.g., photons, ions, superconductors).

- o **Quantum State Representation:** Explain the mathematical notation for qubits and how to visualize their states using the Bloch sphere.

2. **Superposition – The Melodic Blend:**

- o **Mathematical Insight:** Explore the superposition principle and how it enables parallelism in quantum computing.

- o **Examples and Simulations:** Provide examples of superposition in action and how to simulate it using Qiskit.

3. **Entanglement – The Quantum Harmony:**

- o **Entanglement Properties:** Discuss the properties of entangled states and how they are created.

- o **Quantum Applications:** Highlight key applications of entanglement in quantum computing and cryptography.

4. **Measurement – The Final Note:**

- o **Measurement Process:** Explain how measurement collapses the quantum state and the role of probability in quantum mechanics.

- o **Impact on Computation:** Discuss the implications of measurement for quantum algorithms and the challenges it presents.

By the end of this chapter, readers will have a solid understanding of the fundamental principles of quantum computing, setting the foundation for building and analyzing quantum circuits in subsequent chapters.

Chapter 2: Setting Up the Quantum Stage

The First Step: Installing and Configuring Qiskit

Before diving into the depths of quantum algorithms and simulations, it's essential to set up the tools that will enable you to explore the quantum world. In this chapter, we'll guide you through installing and configuring Qiskit, the powerful open-source quantum computing framework developed by IBM.

Analogy: Tuning the Instruments – Preparing Your Quantum Toolkit

Imagine you're about to perform in a grand symphony. Before the concert begins, each musician must tune their instrument to ensure harmony in the performance. Similarly, when embarking on the journey of quantum computing, your first task is to "tune" your quantum instruments—installing and configuring the tools you need to experiment and learn.

1. **The Instruments:**

   - **Qiskit as the Instrument:** Just as musicians need well-tuned instruments to produce beautiful music, quantum developers need Qiskit to explore quantum algorithms. Qiskit serves as the primary tool for creating and manipulating quantum circuits, running quantum algorithms, and interfacing with quantum hardware.

   - **Tuning for Precision:** Just as a musician meticulously tunes their instrument, you must ensure that Qiskit is correctly installed and configured to function seamlessly.

2. **The Orchestra Conductor:**

   - **IBM Quantum Account:** Think of the IBM Quantum account as the conductor that coordinates your quantum experiments. It provides access to IBM's quantum processors and simulators, ensuring that your "music" (quantum experiments) is performed correctly.

Concepts Covered: Qiskit Installation, IBM Quantum Account Setup

1. **Qiskit Installation:**

   - **Introduction to Qiskit:** Qiskit is a comprehensive software development kit (SDK) that enables you to write quantum algorithms, simulate quantum circuits, and run them on real quantum devices. It is designed to be user-friendly and accessible to both beginners and advanced users.

- **Installation Process:**
    - **Prerequisites:** Before installing Qiskit, ensure that Python is installed on your system. Qiskit is compatible with major operating systems, including Windows, macOS, and Linux.
    - **Installation Command:** The installation process is straightforward. You can install Qiskit using pip, Python's package installer. Open your terminal or command prompt and execute the following command:

bash

Code

```
pip install qiskit
```

- **Verifying Installation:** After installation, verify that Qiskit is correctly installed by running a simple Python script. Open a Python environment and execute:

python

Code

```
import qiskit
print("Qiskit installed successfully!")
```

- **Installing Additional Components:** Qiskit includes various components such as Terra, Aer, Ignis, and Aqua. You can install them as needed based on the specific requirements of your quantum experiments.

2. **IBM Quantum Account Setup:**
    - **Creating an IBM Quantum Account:**
        - **Why You Need It:** To run your quantum circuits on real quantum hardware, you'll need an IBM Quantum account. This account gives you access to IBM's cloud-based quantum processors and simulators.

- **Sign-Up Process:** Visit the IBM Quantum Experience website (quantum-computing.ibm.com) and sign up for a free account. Once registered, you'll receive an API token that allows you to connect Qiskit with your IBM Quantum account.

- **Configuring Qiskit with IBM Quantum:**

  - **Connecting Qiskit to Your Account:** After obtaining your API token, configure Qiskit to use it. Open a Python environment and run the following commands:

python

Code

```python
from qiskit import IBMQ

IBMQ.save_account('YOUR_API_TOKEN')
```

- **Loading Your Account:** Each time you want to run quantum circuits on IBM's hardware, you'll need to load your account with the following command:

python

Code

```python
IBMQ.load_account()
```

- **Accessing Quantum Backends:** With your account loaded, you can access various quantum devices and simulators by using:

python

Code

```python
provider = IBMQ.get_provider()

backends = provider.backends()

print(backends)
```

In-Depth Exploration

In this chapter, we delve deeper into the practical aspects of setting up your quantum computing environment. Whether you're a beginner taking your first steps into quantum computing or an experienced developer, mastering these setup processes is crucial.

Detailed Breakdown

1. **Qiskit Installation:**

   o **Troubleshooting:** Learn how to troubleshoot common installation issues, such as conflicts with existing Python packages or system-specific errors.

   o **Upgrading Qiskit:** Discover how to keep your Qiskit installation up to date, ensuring access to the latest features and improvements.

2. **IBM Quantum Account Setup:**

   o **Managing API Tokens:** Understand how to manage your IBM Quantum API tokens, including generating new tokens and revoking old ones.

   o **Accessing Advanced Features:** Explore advanced features of the IBM Quantum Experience, such as setting up quantum jobs, accessing the quantum job queue, and monitoring the status of your quantum experiments.

By the end of this chapter, you'll have a fully configured quantum computing environment, ready to explore the vast potential of quantum algorithms. With Qiskit installed and your IBM Quantum account set up, you'll be well-prepared to embark on the next stage of your quantum journey, where you'll begin crafting your first quantum circuits and running them on real quantum hardware

Chapter 3:
The Quantum
Conductor

Orchestrating a Quantum Circuit

In the world of quantum computing, the quantum circuit is the foundational structure upon which all quantum algorithms are built. Like a piece of music composed of various notes and rhythms, a quantum circuit is composed of qubits and quantum gates. This chapter will guide you through the process of orchestrating a quantum circuit, teaching you how to design and direct the flow of quantum information.

Analogy: The Conductor's Baton – Designing and Directing Quantum Circuits

Imagine a conductor standing before a symphony, baton in hand, ready to bring harmony to the orchestra. The conductor knows exactly when to cue the violins, when to bring in the brass, and when to silence the percussion. Similarly, in quantum computing, you are the conductor of a quantum circuit, using quantum gates to orchestrate the behavior of qubits.

1. **The Instruments (Qubits):**

    o **Qubits as Musical Notes:** Just as a musician plays notes to create a melody, qubits are the fundamental units of quantum circuits. Each qubit can be in a state of 0, 1, or both (superposition), creating the "notes" of your quantum computation.

    o **Entanglement as Harmony:** Entanglement is akin to the harmony between different sections of the orchestra. When qubits are entangled, their states are interconnected, leading to correlations that are essential for complex quantum computations.

2. **The Conductor's Baton (Quantum Gates):**

    o **Quantum Gates as Baton Movements:** The quantum gates are your tools to direct the qubits, just as a conductor uses the baton to guide the orchestra. Each gate you apply modifies the state of the qubits, creating the desired "sound" or output of your quantum circuit.

- ○ **Controlling the Flow:** With each gate, you control the flow of the quantum circuit, deciding when and how qubits should interact. This is the essence of quantum circuit design.

3. **The Final Performance (Measurement):**

   - ○ **Measurement as the Grand Finale:** After orchestrating your quantum circuit, the measurement is the final step—akin to the final note of a symphony. Measurement collapses the quantum states of the qubits into classical bits, providing the output of your quantum computation.

Concepts Covered: Quantum Circuits, Quantum Gates, Measurement

1. **Quantum Circuits:**

   - ○ **What is a Quantum Circuit?** A quantum circuit is a sequence of quantum gates applied to a set of qubits. It's the quantum equivalent of a classical logic circuit, but with far greater complexity due to the principles of superposition and entanglement.

   - ○ **Building Blocks:**

     - ▪ **Qubits:** The basic units that hold quantum information.

     - ▪ **Quantum Gates:** Operations that change the state of qubits.

     - ▪ **Measurement:** The process of reading the final state of the qubits to extract classical information.

2. **Quantum Gates:**

   - ○ **Types of Quantum Gates:**

     - ▪ **Single-Qubit Gates:** These gates operate on a single qubit. Examples include the Pauli-X gate (which flips the qubit state) and the Hadamard gate (which creates superposition).

     - ▪ **Multi-Qubit Gates:** These gates operate on multiple qubits. The most famous is the CNOT gate, which entangles two qubits.

   - ○ **Gate Operations:**

- **Applying Gates:** Learn how to apply quantum gates to qubits to manipulate their states. Each gate corresponds to a matrix operation that alters the qubit's state vector.

- **Circuit Diagrams:** Understand how to represent quantum circuits using circuit diagrams, where qubits are lines and gates are boxes or symbols on these lines.

3. **Measurement:**

   - **Collapsing the Quantum State:** Measurement in quantum computing is the process by which a qubit's state is observed, collapsing it from a superposition to a definite state of 0 or 1.

   - **Interpreting Results:** Learn how to interpret the outcomes of measurements and how these outcomes inform the results of your quantum computation.

   - **Basis States:** Understand the concept of measurement bases, where qubits are measured in specific states (e.g., computational basis states).

In-Depth Exploration

This chapter takes you through the intricacies of designing and implementing quantum circuits. Whether you're simulating on a classical computer or running on actual quantum hardware, mastering the creation and control of quantum circuits is crucial.

Detailed Breakdown

1. **Quantum Circuit Design:**

   - **Circuit Initialization:** Start by initializing your qubits in a known state, typically $|0\rangle$|0\rangle|0\rangle, and apply a series of quantum gates to create the desired quantum state.

   - **Complex Circuits:** Learn how to build more complex circuits that involve multiple qubits and gates, exploring concepts like quantum parallelism and interference.

2. **Applying Quantum Gates:**

- o **Single-Qubit Operations:** Delve deeper into single-qubit gates like the X, Y, Z, Hadamard, and Phase gates. Understand how these gates transform the qubit's state and how to combine them for more complex operations.

- o **Entangling Gates:** Explore the role of multi-qubit gates like the CNOT and Toffoli gates in creating entanglement and performing controlled operations.

3. **Measurement and Post-Processing:**

- o **Measurement Strategies:** Discover different strategies for measuring qubits, including repeated measurements and partial measurements, and how to extract meaningful information from the results.

- o **Interpreting Quantum Data:** Learn how to analyze the results of your quantum circuit, using statistical methods and visualizations to understand the behavior of the quantum system.

By the end of this chapter, you will have a solid understanding of how to design and implement quantum circuits. You'll be equipped to explore more advanced quantum algorithms, build more complex circuits, and deepen your understanding of quantum computation. Just as a conductor brings music to life through careful direction, you will bring quantum circuits to life through careful design and execution.

Chapter 4: The Symphony of Quantum Algorithms

Exploring Quantum Algorithms

Quantum algorithms are the masterpieces of quantum computing, designed to solve complex problems that classical algorithms struggle with or cannot solve efficiently. This chapter delves into some of the most renowned quantum algorithms, exploring how they work and what makes them so powerful. From the Quantum Fourier Transform (QFT) to the Variational Quantum Eigensolver (VQE), you'll uncover the elegance and complexity of these algorithms, understanding their structure, application, and potential impact on various fields.

Analogy: Composing a Masterpiece – How Quantum Algorithms Work

Think of quantum algorithms as symphonies composed by brilliant minds. Each algorithm is a carefully crafted piece of music, where every note, rhythm, and harmony serves a purpose. Just as a composer considers how each instrument contributes to the overall sound, quantum algorithm designers consider how each qubit and gate contributes to solving a problem.

1. **The Theme (Problem to Solve):**

    - **Identifying the Problem:** Just as a composer starts with a theme or idea, quantum algorithms start with a specific problem to solve—whether it's finding the prime factors of a large number, searching through an unsorted database, or estimating the ground state energy of a molecule.

    - **Translating the Theme:** The problem is translated into a quantum framework, where it can be tackled using the unique properties of quantum mechanics.

2. **The Melody (Quantum Fourier Transform - QFT):**

    - **QFT as the Melody:** The Quantum Fourier Transform is a key component in many quantum algorithms, much like a melody is central to a piece of music. It transforms quantum states into a different basis, making patterns or periodicities in the data easier to detect.

- o **Application in Algorithms:** The QFT is crucial in algorithms like Shor's Algorithm for factoring large numbers, where it is used to find the period of a function.

3. **The Harmony (Quantum Phase Estimation - QPE):**

   - o **QPE as Harmony:** Quantum Phase Estimation is like the harmony in music, providing the necessary background that enriches the main theme. QPE is used to estimate the eigenvalues of a unitary operator, which is fundamental in algorithms like Shor's and in applications like quantum chemistry.

   - o **Precision and Structure:** Just as harmony adds depth and structure to music, QPE adds precision and structure to quantum algorithms, allowing for accurate calculations of phases and energy levels.

4. **The Crescendo (Grover's Algorithm):**

   - o **Grover's Algorithm as the Crescendo:** Grover's Algorithm is the powerful, dramatic crescendo in the symphony of quantum algorithms. It amplifies the probability of finding the correct answer in an unsorted database, achieving a quadratic speedup over classical algorithms.

   - o **The Climax:** This algorithm represents the climax where quantum mechanics shows its strength in speeding up certain types of searches.

5. **The Variations (Variational Quantum Eigensolver - VQE, Quantum Approximate Optimization Algorithm - QAOA):**

   - o **VQE and QAOA as Variations:** VQE and QAOA are like variations on a theme, adapting the basic structure of quantum algorithms to tackle optimization problems and estimate ground state energies.

   - o **Adaptive Algorithms:** These algorithms adjust parameters dynamically, akin to how a composer might experiment with different keys or tempos to achieve the desired effect.

Concepts Covered: QFT, QPE, Grover's Algorithm, VQE, QAOA

1. **Quantum Fourier Transform (QFT):**

- **Understanding QFT:** The QFT is a quantum version of the classical Fourier Transform, which decomposes a function into its constituent frequencies. In quantum computing, QFT is used to transform quantum states into a different basis where periodicities are more easily identified.

- **Applications:** QFT is used in algorithms like Shor's for factoring integers, where it helps identify periodicities that are essential for finding the prime factors of a number.

2. **Quantum Phase Estimation (QPE):**

    - **Understanding QPE:** QPE is used to estimate the eigenvalues of a unitary operator, a crucial step in many quantum algorithms. It combines the QFT with controlled unitary operations to extract phase information from quantum states.

    - **Applications:** QPE is fundamental in algorithms like Shor's and in quantum chemistry for calculating molecular energy levels.

3. **Grover's Algorithm:**

    - **Understanding Grover's Algorithm:** Grover's Algorithm provides a quadratic speedup for searching an unsorted database. It repeatedly applies an oracle and a diffusion operator to amplify the probability of finding the correct answer.

    - **Applications:** This algorithm is powerful for database searches, solving problems like finding a specific item in a large dataset more efficiently than classical methods.

4. **Variational Quantum Eigensolver (VQE):**

    - **Understanding VQE:** VQE is a hybrid quantum-classical algorithm used to estimate the ground state energy of a molecule. It involves preparing a quantum state with certain parameters and then using a classical optimizer to minimize the energy expectation value.

    - **Applications:** VQE is widely used in quantum chemistry and materials science to solve problems that are intractable for classical computers.

5. **Quantum Approximate Optimization Algorithm (QAOA):**

- **Understanding QAOA:** QAOA is designed for solving combinatorial optimization problems. It alternates between applying a problem-specific Hamiltonian and a mixing Hamiltonian to find an approximate solution to the optimization problem.

- **Applications:** QAOA is applied to problems like Max-Cut and other NP-hard problems, offering a quantum advantage in finding approximate solutions.

In-Depth Exploration

This chapter provides a deep dive into the mechanics of quantum algorithms. You will explore how these algorithms are constructed, understand their underlying principles, and see how they are applied to solve real-world problems. Through the lens of analogy, these complex concepts become more accessible, allowing you to appreciate the beauty and power of quantum computing.

Detailed Breakdown

1. **Quantum Fourier Transform (QFT):**

   - **Circuit Implementation:** Learn how to implement the QFT in a quantum circuit, including the use of Hadamard gates and controlled phase rotations.

   - **Inverse QFT:** Understand the inverse QFT and its role in reversing the Fourier Transform process, which is critical in algorithms like Shor's.

2. **Quantum Phase Estimation (QPE):**

   - **Step-by-Step Construction:** Follow the step-by-step process of building a QPE circuit, from preparing the initial state to applying the QFT and measuring the output.

   - **Error Mitigation:** Explore techniques for mitigating errors in QPE, such as phase kickback and using ancilla qubits.

3. **Grover's Algorithm:**

- o **Oracle Construction:** Learn how to construct the oracle for Grover's Algorithm, which marks the correct solution within the search space.

- o **Amplitude Amplification:** Understand the process of amplitude amplification, where the probability of the correct solution is increased with each iteration.

4. **Variational Quantum Eigensolver (VQE):**

- o **Ansatz Selection:** Explore different ansatzes (trial wavefunctions) used in VQE, such as the hardware-efficient ansatz and unitary coupled-cluster ansatz.

- o **Classical Optimization:** Delve into the classical optimization process, which tunes the parameters of the quantum circuit to minimize the energy.

5. **Quantum Approximate Optimization Algorithm (QAOA):**

- o **Problem Hamiltonian Design:** Learn how to design the problem Hamiltonian for QAOA, which encodes the problem to be optimized.

- o **Layering Strategy:** Understand how to choose the number of layers (repetition of Hamiltonians) in QAOA to balance between accuracy and computational cost.

By the end of this chapter, you will have a thorough understanding of some of the most important quantum algorithms. You'll see how they can be applied to solve complex problems, pushing the boundaries of what's possible with classical computing. Just as a symphony brings together different instruments to create a masterpiece, quantum algorithms bring together qubits, gates, and measurement to achieve groundbreaking results in computation.

Chapter 5: Simulating the Quantum Symphony

Simulating Quantum Circuits

Before running quantum algorithms on actual quantum hardware, it's often beneficial to simulate them. Simulation allows you to test and refine your quantum circuits in a controlled environment, helping to identify and fix issues before they arise in a real quantum system. This chapter will introduce you to the concept of quantum circuit simulation using Qiskit Aer, a powerful tool for simulating quantum circuits and algorithms. You'll learn how to use simulation to validate your quantum circuits, analyze their behavior, and ensure they perform as expected.

Analogy: The Dress Rehearsal – Testing Quantum Circuits in Simulation

Imagine you're preparing for a grand symphony performance. Before stepping onto the stage, you conduct a dress rehearsal to ensure every instrument is in tune, every musician knows their part, and the entire orchestra can perform flawlessly. In quantum computing, simulating quantum circuits is akin to this dress rehearsal. It's your opportunity to test and refine your quantum circuits before running them on real quantum hardware.

1. **Tuning the Instruments (Calibrating the Simulation):**

    o **Precision and Accuracy:** Just as you would ensure each instrument is finely tuned, you calibrate your quantum simulation to accurately reflect the behavior of a quantum computer. This involves setting the parameters for noise models, gate fidelities, and measurement errors to simulate real-world conditions.

2. **Rehearsing the Performance (Running the Simulation):**

    o **Step-by-Step Execution:** During the dress rehearsal, each part of the symphony is played through, checking for harmony and timing. Similarly, in quantum simulation, you run your quantum circuits step by step, observing the outcomes at each stage. This allows you to detect any issues or unexpected behaviors that could disrupt the final performance.

3. **Identifying and Fixing Issues (Debugging the Circuit):**

    o **Refinement:** If the rehearsal reveals any discord or mistakes, you have the chance to correct them before the performance. In quantum simulation, you can debug and modify your circuits, ensuring they are optimized and error-free before being run on actual quantum hardware.

4. **Final Run-Through (Optimizing the Simulation):**

   o **Optimization for Real Hardware:** The final run-through of the rehearsal ensures everything is perfect for the big day. In quantum simulation, this means fine-tuning your circuits for efficiency and performance, preparing them for the real quantum environment.

Concepts Covered: Qiskit Aer, Simulation of Quantum Circuits

1. **Qiskit Aer:**

   o **Introduction to Qiskit Aer:** Qiskit Aer is a powerful simulator for quantum circuits, enabling you to simulate the behavior of quantum algorithms on classical hardware. Aer allows you to model quantum noise, visualize quantum states, and analyze circuit performance in a flexible and efficient manner.

   o **Components of Qiskit Aer:** Explore the various components of Qiskit Aer, including statevector simulators, unitary simulators, and noise simulators, each serving a different purpose in the simulation process.

2. **Simulation of Quantum Circuits:**

   o **Running Simulations:** Learn how to run quantum circuit simulations using Qiskit Aer. This includes setting up your simulation environment, choosing the appropriate simulator, and executing quantum circuits to obtain results.

   o **Analyzing Results:** Understand how to analyze the output of quantum simulations, including statevectors, probabilities, and measurement outcomes. This analysis helps you understand how your quantum circuit behaves and where improvements can be made.

3. **Noise Modeling and Error Simulation:**

   o **Simulating Noise:** In the real world, quantum computers are subject to various noise sources that can affect the accuracy of computations. Qiskit Aer allows you to model these noise sources in simulation, helping you understand how your circuits will perform under realistic conditions.

- o **Error Mitigation Techniques:** Learn about error mitigation techniques that can be applied during simulation to reduce the impact of noise and improve the accuracy of your quantum computations.

4. **Optimization and Scalability:**

- o **Circuit Optimization:** Discover techniques for optimizing quantum circuits during simulation, including gate decomposition, circuit depth reduction, and qubit reuse strategies. These optimizations help make your circuits more efficient and scalable for real quantum hardware.

- o **Scalability Considerations:** Understand the challenges of scaling quantum circuits for larger problems, and how simulation can help identify potential bottlenecks and performance issues.

In-Depth Exploration

This chapter provides a comprehensive guide to simulating quantum circuits using Qiskit Aer. You'll explore the capabilities of Qiskit Aer, learn how to set up and run simulations, and gain insights into how your quantum circuits will perform on actual quantum hardware. Through the analogy of a dress rehearsal, you'll appreciate the importance of simulation in the quantum development process, ensuring that your circuits are well-prepared for their real-world debut.

Detailed Breakdown

1. **Setting Up Qiskit Aer:**

- o **Installation and Configuration:** Learn how to install and configure Qiskit Aer as part of your quantum computing environment.

- o **Choosing the Right Simulator:** Understand the different types of simulators available in Qiskit Aer, and how to choose the one that best fits your needs.

2. **Simulating Quantum Circuits:**

- o **Building a Circuit:** Follow a step-by-step guide to building a quantum circuit and running it on a Qiskit Aer simulator. Explore the use of statevector simulators for analyzing quantum states, and noise simulators for testing circuits under realistic conditions.

- o **Visualizing Quantum States:** Learn how to visualize the quantum states produced by your circuit, including statevector plots, Bloch sphere representations, and probability distributions.

3. **Debugging and Refining Circuits:**

- o **Identifying Errors:** Explore common errors that can occur in quantum circuits and how to detect them during simulation. Learn techniques for debugging circuits and improving their reliability.

- o **Circuit Optimization:** Discover methods for optimizing your quantum circuits, such as minimizing gate counts, reducing circuit depth, and optimizing qubit layouts for specific hardware architectures.

4. **Preparing for Real Hardware Execution:**

- o **Noise Modeling:** Understand the importance of simulating noise and how to model different types of noise (e.g., depolarizing noise, amplitude damping) in Qiskit Aer.

- o **Error Mitigation:** Learn about error mitigation strategies that can be applied during simulation to enhance the accuracy and robustness of your quantum circuits.

By the end of this chapter, you will have a thorough understanding of how to simulate quantum circuits using Qiskit Aer. You'll be able to build, test, and optimize quantum circuits in a simulated environment, ensuring they are ready for execution on real quantum hardware. This preparation is crucial for successful quantum computing, much like a flawless dress rehearsal is essential for a perfect performance.

Chapter 6: Performing on the Quantum Stage

Running Circuits on Real Quantum Hardware

After thorough simulation and testing, the next step in your quantum journey is to execute your circuits on real quantum hardware. This chapter will guide you through the process of running your quantum circuits on IBM's quantum computers using Qiskit. You will learn how to connect to IBM Quantum devices, submit jobs, retrieve results, and analyze the performance of your quantum algorithms on actual quantum processors.

Analogy: The Live Performance – Running Quantum Circuits on Real Devices

Imagine you've completed all your rehearsals, fine-tuned every note, and now it's time for the live performance. The anticipation is high, the audience is waiting, and everything must go perfectly. Running quantum circuits on real quantum hardware is similar to this live performance. It's the moment when all your preparation culminates in a real-world execution, where the nuances of quantum mechanics come into play, and the results reflect the true nature of quantum computation.

1. **The Curtain Rises (Connecting to IBM Quantum Devices):**

   o **Accessing the Stage:** Just as you step onto the stage to begin your performance, in quantum computing, you connect to IBM Quantum devices. This involves setting up your IBM Quantum account, accessing available quantum computers, and preparing to run your circuits in a real quantum environment.

2. **The Performance Begins (Executing Quantum Circuits):**

   o **Submitting Jobs:** With the audience watching, you begin your performance by submitting quantum circuits to the selected quantum hardware. In this context, you send your quantum jobs to IBMQ devices, where they are queued and executed.

   o **Handling Real-World Variability:** In a live performance, unexpected variables like acoustics or audience reactions can affect the outcome. Similarly, in quantum computing, real hardware introduces factors like noise, decoherence, and gate errors, which can influence the results.

3. **The Applause (Retrieving and Analyzing Results):**

   o **Collecting Feedback:** After the performance, the applause and audience feedback reflect how well the symphony was received. In quantum computing, this is akin to retrieving and analyzing the results of your quantum computations. You interpret the output data, assess the performance of your circuit, and make conclusions based on real-world quantum behavior.

4. **Learning from the Experience (Refining and Iterating):**

   o **Improving Future Performances:** Every live performance provides insights that can be used to improve future shows.

Similarly, running quantum circuits on real hardware offers valuable feedback that you can use to refine your algorithms, adjust parameters, and prepare for more complex quantum computations.

Concepts Covered: IBMQ, Real Quantum Hardware Execution

1. **Connecting to IBMQ:**

   o **Setting Up IBMQ:** Learn how to set up and configure your IBM Quantum account to access real quantum devices. This includes obtaining your API token, connecting to the IBMQ provider in Qiskit, and viewing the available quantum backends.

   o **Choosing the Right Backend:** Understand how to select the appropriate quantum device for your needs, considering factors like qubit count, noise levels, and queue times. Explore the differences between various IBMQ backends, including their capabilities and limitations.

2. **Executing Quantum Circuits:**

   o **Submitting Jobs to Quantum Hardware:** Follow a step-by-step guide on how to submit your quantum circuits to real quantum devices. Learn how to monitor the job queue, understand the execution process, and retrieve the results once the job is completed.

   o **Dealing with Noise and Errors:** Explore the impact of noise and errors in real quantum hardware and how they can affect your results. Learn about techniques for mitigating these issues, such as error correction and post-processing.

3. **Analyzing Results:**

   o **Interpreting Quantum Data:** Discover how to analyze the results returned by the quantum hardware. This includes understanding the output formats, calculating probabilities, and comparing the results with your expectations based on simulations.

   o **Benchmarking Quantum Performance:** Learn how to benchmark the performance of your quantum circuits on real hardware, including measuring gate fidelities, coherence times, and overall circuit reliability.

4. **Iterating and Refining:**

   o **Feedback Loop:** Understand the importance of iterating on your quantum circuits based on the results from real hardware. Learn how to refine your algorithms, adjust for hardware-specific issues, and optimize your circuits for better performance in future executions.

   o **Preparing for Advanced Quantum Computing:** As you gain experience running circuits on real quantum hardware, you'll be better prepared to tackle more complex quantum algorithms and explore the frontier of quantum computing.

In-Depth Exploration

This chapter provides a comprehensive guide to executing quantum circuits on real quantum hardware. Through the analogy of a live performance, you'll understand the significance of this step in the quantum development process. You'll learn how to connect to IBM Quantum devices, submit and execute quantum jobs, and analyze the results to gain insights into the true behavior of your quantum circuits.

Detailed Breakdown

1. **Setting Up IBM Quantum Access:**

   o **Account Setup:** Learn how to create and configure your IBM Quantum account, including generating your API token and linking it with Qiskit.

   o **Choosing Quantum Devices:** Explore the various quantum backends available through IBMQ, understanding their specifications and how to choose the best one for your project.

2. **Running Quantum Circuits:**

   o **Job Submission:** Follow a practical guide on how to submit quantum circuits to real quantum hardware, including code examples and tips for efficient execution.

   o **Understanding Real Hardware Execution:** Delve into the intricacies of running circuits on real quantum devices, including the role of quantum gates, decoherence, and how hardware limitations can influence your results.

3. **Analyzing and Interpreting Results:**

   o **Result Retrieval:** Learn how to retrieve and interpret the results from quantum hardware, including probability distributions, bitstring outputs, and statevectors.

   o **Performance Analysis:** Understand how to assess the performance of your circuits on real quantum hardware, including metrics like success rates, error rates, and overall circuit fidelity.

4. **Refining Quantum Circuits:**

   o **Error Mitigation and Correction:** Explore techniques for mitigating errors and improving the accuracy of your quantum computations, including post-processing methods and error correction codes.

   o **Optimizing for Real Hardware:** Learn strategies for optimizing your quantum circuits for specific quantum devices, including reducing circuit depth, minimizing qubit usage, and optimizing gate sequences.

By the end of this chapter, you will have the knowledge and skills to confidently run quantum circuits on real quantum hardware. You'll understand the challenges and opportunities that come with working on actual quantum devices and be prepared to refine your circuits for more complex and ambitious quantum computations.

Chapter 7: Interpreting the Quantum Melody

Analyzing Quantum Circuit Results

After successfully running your quantum circuits on real hardware, the next critical step is analyzing the results. This chapter delves into the process of interpreting the outcomes of quantum computations, helping you make sense of the measurement data, probability distributions, and error patterns you encounter. Understanding these results is crucial for refining your quantum algorithms and improving their performance on both simulated and real quantum devices.

Analogy: Reading the Audience – Interpreting the Outcomes of Quantum Computations

Imagine you've just finished a live performance, and now you're observing the audience's reactions. Their applause, expressions, and feedback provide valuable insights into how well your performance resonated with them. Similarly, when working with quantum circuits, the measurement results and probability distributions are like the audience's feedback—offering you clues about how well your quantum "performance" (computation) went. The challenge lies in correctly interpreting this feedback to improve future performances.

1. **The Applause (Measurement Results):**

   o **Understanding the Feedback:** Just as applause indicates the audience's reaction, the measurement results from your quantum circuits tell you how the quantum system behaved during computation. Each measurement reflects the final state of qubits after executing the quantum circuit, offering insights into the probability distribution of possible outcomes.

2. **Decoding the Reactions (Probability Distributions):**

   o **Interpreting Probabilities:** The way different outcomes are distributed across measurements is akin to reading the varied reactions of an audience. In quantum computing, probability distributions reveal the likelihood of each possible outcome, helping you understand which states were most prominent in the computation.

3. **Identifying Areas for Improvement (Error Analysis):**

   o **Spotting Flaws:** Just as you might notice areas where the performance could improve, error analysis in quantum computing helps identify sources of inaccuracy. These could include noise, decoherence, or gate errors that skew the results. By analyzing these errors, you can refine your quantum circuits to achieve better accuracy.

4. **Refining the Act (Iterative Improvement):**

   o **Preparing for the Next Performance:** Armed with insights from the audience's feedback, you refine your performance for the next show. Similarly, after interpreting quantum results, you can adjust your circuits, implement error correction techniques, and improve the overall design to enhance future computations.

Concepts Covered: Measurement Results, Probability Distributions, Error Analysis

1. **Understanding Measurement Results:**

   o **Measurement in Quantum Circuits:** Learn how quantum measurements collapse qubits' superposition into definite states, producing bitstrings that represent the outcome of your quantum computation. Explore how these measurements are recorded and how to interpret the raw data returned by quantum hardware.

   o **Interpreting Bitstrings:** Understand how to read and analyze the bitstrings produced by quantum measurements. Each bitstring corresponds to a specific outcome, and their frequency across multiple runs provides information on the probability distribution of quantum states.

2. **Interpreting Probability Distributions:**

   o **Probability in Quantum Mechanics:** Explore the concept of probability distributions in quantum computing. Learn how to extract and visualize these distributions from measurement results, and how they reflect the quantum state's behavior throughout the circuit.

   o **Expectation Values and Their Significance:** Discover how to calculate expectation values for observables, which provide a statistical average of measurement outcomes. These values are crucial for understanding the overall performance and reliability of your quantum circuits.

3. **Analyzing and Mitigating Errors:**

   o **Identifying Sources of Error:** Learn about the common sources of errors in quantum computations, including gate imperfections, decoherence, and environmental noise. Understand how these errors manifest in the results and how to detect them through careful analysis.

- o **Error Mitigation Techniques:** Explore various methods for mitigating errors in quantum circuits, such as error correction codes, post-processing techniques, and circuit optimizations. These techniques help improve the accuracy and reliability of your quantum computations.

4. **Refining Quantum Circuits:**

- o **Iterative Improvement:** Understand the importance of refining and iterating on quantum circuits based on the insights gained from result analysis. Learn how to adjust your circuit design, choose more suitable quantum gates, and implement error correction strategies to enhance future computations.

- o **Preparing for Advanced Quantum Challenges:** As you become proficient in interpreting quantum results, you'll be better equipped to tackle more complex quantum algorithms and experiments, ultimately contributing to the advancement of quantum computing.

In-Depth Exploration

This chapter provides a detailed guide to interpreting the results of quantum circuits, drawing parallels with understanding audience reactions in a performance. By the end of this chapter, you'll be able to confidently analyze quantum measurement data, understand the significance of probability distributions, and apply error analysis to refine your quantum circuits.

Detailed Breakdown

1. **Measurement Results:**

- o **Quantum Measurement Process:** Gain a deep understanding of how quantum measurements collapse qubits' superpositions and how these measurements translate into classical bitstrings.

- o **Bitstring Analysis:** Learn how to analyze the bitstrings returned by quantum hardware, understanding their implications for the final quantum state.

2. **Probability Distributions:**

- **Visualizing Distributions:** Explore tools and techniques for visualizing probability distributions of quantum states, helping you see which outcomes are most likely.

- **Interpreting Results:** Understand how to interpret these distributions to assess the effectiveness of your quantum algorithms and identify areas for improvement.

3. **Error Analysis:**

- **Error Sources in Quantum Circuits:** Delve into the various sources of errors in quantum computations, including hardware imperfections and environmental factors.

- **Mitigation Strategies:** Learn practical strategies for mitigating these errors, including using redundancy, adjusting gate sequences, and applying error correction methods.

4. **Circuit Refinement:**

- **Refining Based on Analysis:** Discover how to refine your quantum circuits based on the insights gained from result analysis, improving accuracy and preparing for more complex challenges.

- **Preparing for Future Research:** Equip yourself with the skills needed to push the boundaries of quantum computing, contributing to research and development in this rapidly evolving field.

By mastering the art of interpreting quantum results, you'll gain the ability to fine-tune your quantum circuits, reduce errors, and achieve more reliable outcomes. This chapter lays the foundation for deeper exploration into advanced quantum algorithms and prepares you for the challenges of real-world quantum computing.

Chapter 8: Tuning the Quantum Orchestra

Optimizing and Improving Quantum Circuits

As you dive deeper into the quantum realm, the need for optimization becomes paramount. Quantum circuits, much like musical compositions, require fine-tuning to achieve the best possible performance. This chapter focuses on the art and science of optimizing quantum circuits, mitigating errors, and implementing advanced techniques to enhance the efficiency and reliability of quantum computations.

Analogy: Fine-Tuning the Instruments – Optimizing Quantum Solutions

Imagine an orchestra preparing for a grand performance. Even with skilled musicians and a well-composed piece, the instruments need meticulous tuning to produce a harmonious sound. Similarly, in quantum computing, your circuits—no matter how well-designed—require optimization to minimize noise, reduce errors, and maximize computational efficiency.

1. **Tuning the Strings (Circuit Optimization):**

   o **Balancing the Frequencies:** Just as a violinist tightens or loosens the strings to achieve the perfect pitch, you must optimize your quantum circuits to balance gate operations, reduce circuit depth, and minimize noise. This fine-tuning ensures that your circuits perform at their best on quantum hardware.

2. **Reducing Background Noise (Error Mitigation):**

   o **Filtering Out Disturbances:** In an orchestra, background noise can ruin the performance. In quantum computing, errors and noise can distort the results. Implementing error mitigation techniques is like applying filters to reduce these disturbances, allowing the true melody of your quantum algorithm to shine through.

3. **Advanced Techniques (Enhancing the Performance):**

   o **Mastering the Art:** Just as advanced musicians might use special techniques to add flair to their performance, quantum computing offers advanced techniques like dynamic decoupling, pulse-level control, and error correction codes. These methods enhance the performance of your circuits, pushing the boundaries of what's possible in quantum computation.

4. **Harmonizing the Ensemble (Integrated Optimization):**

   o **Bringing It All Together:** In an orchestra, the conductor ensures that all instruments play in harmony. In quantum computing, integrated optimization strategies ensure that various parts of your quantum circuit work together seamlessly, reducing redundancy and improving overall efficiency.

Concepts Covered: Circuit Optimization, Error Mitigation, Advanced Techniques

1. **Circuit Optimization:**

   o **Minimizing Circuit Depth:** Learn how to reduce the depth of quantum circuits by minimizing the number of gate operations, which helps decrease the likelihood of errors and improve execution time.

   o **Gate-Level Optimization:** Explore techniques for optimizing individual quantum gates, such as combining or reordering gates to reduce error rates and enhance performance.

   o **Resource Management:** Understand how to optimize the use of quantum resources, such as qubits and gate operations, to achieve more efficient and scalable circuits.

2. **Error Mitigation:**

   o **Noise Reduction Techniques:** Discover methods to reduce the impact of noise on quantum computations, including techniques like zero-noise extrapolation and probabilistic error cancellation.

   o **Error Mitigation Strategies:** Explore strategies for mitigating errors in quantum circuits, such as using redundant qubits, implementing error detection mechanisms, and applying quantum error correction codes.

   o **Post-Processing Adjustments:** Learn how to apply post-processing techniques to correct for errors in measurement results, improving the accuracy of quantum computations.

3. **Advanced Techniques:**

   o **Pulse-Level Control:** Delve into pulse-level control techniques that allow for fine-tuned manipulation of quantum gates at the hardware level, leading to more precise and efficient quantum operations.

   o **Dynamic Decoupling:** Explore dynamic decoupling techniques that protect qubits from decoherence by strategically applying sequences of pulses to counteract environmental noise.

- o **Error Correction Codes:** Understand the principles of quantum error correction codes, which provide a robust framework for detecting and correcting errors in quantum computations, enabling more reliable quantum systems.

4. **Integrated Optimization:**

- o **Holistic Circuit Design:** Learn how to design quantum circuits with integrated optimization strategies that consider all aspects of the computation, from gate operations to error correction, to achieve the best possible performance.

- o **Cross-Layer Optimization:** Explore cross-layer optimization techniques that involve collaboration between different layers of the quantum computing stack, from hardware to software, to enhance the overall efficiency and accuracy of quantum circuits.

- o **Iterative Refinement:** Understand the importance of iterative refinement in optimizing quantum circuits, allowing you to continuously improve your designs based on performance feedback and error analysis.

In-Depth Exploration

This chapter provides a comprehensive guide to optimizing quantum circuits, using the analogy of tuning musical instruments to illustrate the importance of precision and care in quantum computing. By the end of this chapter, you'll have the knowledge and tools to fine-tune your quantum circuits, mitigate errors, and apply advanced techniques to push the boundaries of quantum computation.

Detailed Breakdown

1. **Circuit Optimization:**

- o **Reducing Gate Operations:** Learn specific techniques for minimizing the number of gate operations in your circuits, which directly impacts the circuit's overall performance and error rates.

- o **Optimizing Circuit Layout:** Explore strategies for optimizing the layout of quantum circuits, including qubit placement and connectivity, to reduce the need for complex operations and improve overall efficiency.

2. **Error Mitigation:**

   o **Advanced Noise Reduction:** Delve into advanced noise reduction techniques that go beyond basic error correction, including machine learning approaches to predict and compensate for noise in quantum computations.

   o **Error Mitigation Frameworks:** Discover frameworks for implementing error mitigation strategies in quantum circuits, allowing for scalable and automated error reduction across various quantum systems.

3. **Advanced Techniques:**

   o **Pulse-Level Programming:** Gain hands-on experience with pulse-level programming, which allows for more granular control over quantum operations, leading to more precise and efficient quantum gates.

   o **Quantum Error Correction Implementation:** Learn how to implement quantum error correction codes in real quantum circuits, including the challenges and considerations involved in protecting quantum information from errors.

4. **Integrated Optimization:**

   o **Holistic Approach to Circuit Design:** Understand how to approach quantum circuit design holistically, considering all aspects of the computation to achieve the best possible performance.

   o **Iterative Refinement and Feedback Loops:** Explore the concept of iterative refinement and feedback loops in quantum circuit optimization, allowing for continuous improvement and adaptation to changing conditions.

By mastering the techniques covered in this chapter, you'll be equipped to optimize and fine-tune quantum circuits, ensuring that your quantum computations are as efficient, accurate, and reliable as possible. This chapter sets the stage for more advanced quantum challenges and prepares you to tackle complex quantum algorithms with confidence.

Chapter 9: The Quantum Encore

Deploying and Sharing Quantum Solutions

After you've crafted, optimized, and perfected your quantum circuits, the final step is to share your work with the world. This chapter focuses on deploying your quantum solutions, sharing them with the community, and contributing to the open-source ecosystem that drives innovation in quantum computing. Just as a musician performs their masterpiece before an audience, a quantum developer must present their work to peers and collaborators, ensuring that their contributions can be utilized, built upon, and celebrated.

Analogy: The Curtain Call – Sharing Your Quantum Masterpiece with the World

Imagine the final note of a symphony reverberating through a concert hall, followed by the silence before the applause. The conductor turns to the audience, acknowledging the collective effort that brought the music to life. In the world of quantum computing, this moment of recognition corresponds to deploying and sharing your quantum solutions. Your work is the result of meticulous design, rigorous testing, and creative innovation, and now it's time to take a bow and share it with the broader community.

1. **Preparing for the Curtain Call (Deploying Solutions):**

   o **Final Rehearsals:** Before a live performance, musicians rehearse extensively. Similarly, you must ensure your quantum solutions are thoroughly tested and validated before deployment. This includes checking for errors, optimizing for performance, and preparing for real-world execution.

2. **The Final Performance (Deploying on Quantum Hardware):**

   o **Taking the Stage:** Just as a live performance requires careful coordination, deploying quantum solutions involves executing your quantum circuits on real hardware. This step requires a deep understanding of the quantum devices you're targeting, ensuring compatibility and optimal performance.

3. **Sharing the Masterpiece (Open Source Contributions):**

   o **Opening the Doors:** Once the performance is complete, musicians often share their music with the world through recordings and sheet music. In quantum computing, you can share your solutions by contributing to open-source repositories, allowing others to learn from, use, and build upon your work.

4. **Engaging with the Audience (Community Contributions):**

   o **Inviting Applause and Feedback:** Just as a performance isn't complete without audience engagement, your quantum work benefits from community interaction. By sharing your solutions, you invite feedback, collaboration, and new ideas, helping to push the boundaries of what's possible in quantum computing.

Concepts Covered: Deploying Solutions, Sharing with the Community, Open Source Contributions

1. **Deploying Solutions:**

   - **Preparation for Deployment:** Understand the key steps involved in preparing your quantum circuits for deployment, including final optimization, error checking, and performance validation.

   - **Deployment on Quantum Hardware:** Learn how to execute your quantum solutions on real quantum devices, including selecting the appropriate hardware, managing resource constraints, and optimizing for specific hardware characteristics.

   - **Monitoring and Maintenance:** Explore techniques for monitoring the performance of your deployed quantum circuits, including troubleshooting common issues and ensuring ongoing reliability.

2. **Sharing with the Community:**

   - **Open Source Contributions:** Discover how to contribute your quantum solutions to open-source repositories, including best practices for documentation, code sharing, and collaboration.

   - **Community Engagement:** Learn how to engage with the quantum computing community, including participating in forums, attending conferences, and collaborating on open-source projects.

   - **Showcasing Your Work:** Explore methods for showcasing your quantum solutions to a broader audience, including writing blog posts, giving presentations, and creating tutorials.

3. **Open Source Contributions:**

   - **Building on Open-Source Platforms:** Understand the importance of open-source in the quantum computing ecosystem, and learn how to leverage existing open-source tools and libraries to enhance your work.

   - **Contributing to Quantum Projects:** Explore opportunities to contribute to ongoing quantum computing projects, including adding features, fixing bugs, and collaborating with other developers.

   - **Creating New Open-Source Projects:** Learn how to create and maintain your own open-source quantum computing projects, including setting up repositories, managing contributions, and fostering a community around your work.

In-Depth Exploration

This chapter is your guide to taking your quantum solutions beyond the confines of your own work and into the broader quantum community. By the end of this chapter, you'll be equipped with the knowledge and tools to deploy your quantum circuits on real hardware, share your work with others, and contribute to the vibrant, collaborative ecosystem that is advancing the field of quantum computing.

Detailed Breakdown

1. **Deploying Solutions:**

   o **Final Preparations:** Learn about the critical final steps before deployment, including running extensive tests, optimizing for the target hardware, and ensuring that your quantum solutions are ready for real-world execution.

   o **Deploying on Quantum Hardware:** Dive into the process of deploying quantum circuits on actual quantum hardware, understanding the challenges and best practices for achieving successful execution.

   o **Post-Deployment Monitoring:** Explore methods for monitoring your deployed quantum solutions, including detecting and addressing performance issues, and ensuring that your circuits continue to operate as expected.

2. **Sharing with the Community:**

   o **Open Source Best Practices:** Gain insights into best practices for contributing to open-source quantum computing projects, including how to structure your code, write clear documentation, and engage with other contributors.

   o **Engaging with Quantum Communities:** Learn how to become an active participant in the quantum computing community, including finding and joining relevant forums, attending conferences, and collaborating on open-source projects.

- o **Showcasing Your Quantum Work:** Discover strategies for effectively showcasing your quantum computing solutions, including creating engaging presentations, writing insightful blog posts, and developing educational tutorials.

3. **Open Source Contributions:**

   - o **Leveraging Open Source:** Understand the value of open-source tools and libraries in quantum computing, and learn how to incorporate them into your own work to enhance efficiency and innovation.

   - o **Contributing to Existing Projects:** Explore the opportunities and responsibilities involved in contributing to existing open-source quantum computing projects, including understanding project governance, following contribution guidelines, and collaborating with other developers.

   - o **Creating and Leading Open Source Projects:** Learn how to create and manage your own open-source quantum computing projects, including setting up repositories, managing contributions, and building a community around your work.

By mastering the concepts covered in this chapter, you'll be ready to take your place in the quantum computing community, sharing your work, collaborating with others, and contributing to the ongoing advancement of this exciting field. The curtain has fallen on your personal journey, but the encore—where you share your quantum masterpiece with the world—has just begun.

Chapter 10: The Future of Quantum Symphony

Looking Ahead in Quantum Computing

As you stand at the end of your journey through the world of quantum computing, it's time to look ahead at the evolving landscape of this groundbreaking field. Quantum computing is still in its infancy, with immense potential waiting to be unlocked. This chapter explores the emerging trends, the concept of quantum supremacy, and what the future holds for Qiskit and the quantum computing ecosystem. Just as a composer envisions the next great symphony, we must envision the future of quantum solutions, understanding that today's innovations are just the beginning.

Analogy: The Next Composition – The Future of Quantum Solutions

Imagine a composer who has just completed a symphony, yet is already thinking about the next masterpiece. The final note of one composition doesn't signify an end, but rather a new beginning—a stepping stone to what comes next. In quantum computing, every advancement, discovery, and solution we develop today paves the way for future innovations. Just as the composer is inspired by past works to create something new, quantum researchers and developers will draw on today's achievements to push the boundaries of what's possible in quantum computing.

1. **Envisioning the Next Masterpiece (Emerging Trends):**

   o **New Movements in Quantum Music:** Just as musical styles evolve, so too does quantum computing. Emerging trends like quantum machine learning, quantum cryptography, and hybrid quantum-classical algorithms are shaping the future of the field.

   o **Innovation in Instruments (Hardware Advances):** The instruments of quantum computing—quantum processors, error-correcting codes, and quantum networking—are rapidly evolving, much like the development of new musical instruments that expand the possibilities of sound.

2. **Quantum Supremacy (The Peak of Performance):**

   o **Achieving the Unimaginable:** Quantum supremacy, the point at which quantum computers can solve problems beyond the reach of classical computers, represents a pinnacle moment in the field, much like a composer breaking new ground with a revolutionary symphony.

   o **The Road to Supremacy:** While quantum supremacy has been demonstrated in specific cases, the journey to making it practical and widespread is ongoing. This quest mirrors the effort required to bring an avant-garde musical composition to life.

3. **The Future of Qiskit (The Next Toolkit for Quantum Composers):**

   o **Qiskit's Role in the Future:** Qiskit, like a versatile musical toolkit, will continue to evolve, incorporating new algorithms, tools, and features that will empower quantum developers to create more sophisticated and powerful quantum solutions.

   o **Open Source and Community Growth:** The future of Qiskit is not just in the hands of its creators, but also the global community of quantum enthusiasts who contribute to its development. This collaborative growth will drive innovation, just as a symphony orchestra evolves through the contributions of each musician.

Concepts Covered: Emerging Trends, Quantum Supremacy, Future of Qiskit

1. **Emerging Trends:**

   o **Quantum Machine Learning:** Discover how quantum computing is beginning to revolutionize machine learning by providing new ways to process and analyze vast datasets.

   o **Quantum Cryptography:** Explore the advancements in quantum cryptography, which promises to make communications virtually unbreakable through quantum key distribution and other techniques.

   o **Hybrid Quantum-Classical Algorithms:** Learn about the development of algorithms that combine the strengths of both quantum and classical computing, creating powerful new solutions for complex problems.

2. **Quantum Supremacy:**

   o **Understanding Quantum Supremacy:** Gain insights into what quantum supremacy means, the significance of its achievement, and the ongoing challenges in realizing its full potential.

   o **Practical Implications:** Explore the practical implications of quantum supremacy for industries such as pharmaceuticals, materials science, and finance, where quantum computers may soon outperform classical counterparts.

3. **Future of Qiskit:**

   o **Qiskit's Evolution:** Delve into the future roadmap for Qiskit, including planned updates, new features, and enhancements that will continue to empower developers in building advanced quantum solutions.

   o **Community Contributions:** Understand the importance of the open-source community in shaping the future of Qiskit, and learn how you can contribute to its ongoing development and success.

In-Depth Exploration

This chapter serves as a forward-looking conclusion to your journey in quantum computing. It provides a glimpse into the exciting future of the field, the challenges that lie ahead, and the opportunities for continued innovation and exploration. By the end of this chapter, you'll not only have a solid understanding of the current state of quantum computing but also a clear vision of where the field is headed and how you can be a part of its future.

Detailed Breakdown

1. **Emerging Trends:**

   o **Quantum Machine Learning:** Learn how quantum computing is set to transform the field of machine learning, enabling faster, more efficient processing of complex datasets and opening new avenues for AI research.

   o **Quantum Cryptography:** Explore the cutting-edge advancements in quantum cryptography, including quantum key distribution, quantum-safe encryption, and their implications for data security.

   o **Hybrid Algorithms:** Understand how hybrid quantum-classical algorithms are becoming a critical part of quantum computing, combining the best of both worlds to solve problems that are currently beyond the reach of either paradigm alone.

2. **Quantum Supremacy:**

   o **Defining Supremacy:** Understand the technical and theoretical underpinnings of quantum supremacy, including how it is measured, the benchmarks used, and the significance of achieving it.

   o **Challenges Ahead:** Explore the challenges that still need to be addressed before quantum supremacy can be realized in practical, real-world applications, including scalability, error correction, and hardware limitations.

3. **Future of Qiskit:**

   o **Upcoming Features:** Discover the new features and updates planned for Qiskit, including enhancements to existing tools, the introduction of new algorithms, and improvements to user experience.

   o **Community Involvement:** Learn about the ways in which the Qiskit community contributes to the platform's evolution, including contributing code, providing feedback, and participating in collaborative projects.

As you close this chapter, you'll find yourself at the forefront of quantum computing, equipped with the knowledge, tools, and vision to contribute to the next wave of quantum innovations. The future of quantum computing is bright, and your journey is far from over—it's just beginning. The next composition is waiting to be written, and the quantum symphony will continue to evolve with each new discovery and contribution from pioneers like you.

The Future of Quantum Symphony

Looking Ahead in Quantum Computing

Just as a symphony composer envisions future compositions, quantum computing is evolving, with new trends, ideas, and tools emerging every day. This chapter is about how we can build the future of quantum computing using Qiskit, and what possibilities lie ahead.

Analogy: The Next Composition – The Future of Quantum Solutions

Think of quantum computing as a musical journey. Every innovation, like a new symphony, starts with understanding and builds upon what came before. The more we explore, the more we can create new "musical compositions" in the quantum realm.

1. **Envisioning the Next Masterpiece (Emerging Trends):**
   o **New Movements in Quantum Music:** Just as music has genres, quantum computing has emerging trends like quantum machine learning and quantum cryptography. These are like new styles of music that open up different ways of expressing ideas.

- - **Innovation in Instruments (Hardware Advances):** The quantum processors and tools we use are like the instruments in an orchestra. As these instruments improve, the music we can create becomes more complex and beautiful.

2. **Quantum Supremacy (The Peak of Performance):**

   - **Achieving the Unimaginable:** Quantum supremacy is like composing a piece of music so complex and beautiful that no traditional orchestra could ever play it. It represents the point where quantum computers solve problems that classical computers cannot.

   - **The Road to Supremacy:** Just like it takes time to master a new musical technique, achieving practical quantum supremacy is a journey. It requires overcoming many challenges, but the reward is a completely new way of solving problems.

3. **The Future of Qiskit (The Next Toolkit for Quantum Composers):**

   - **Qiskit's Role in the Future:** Qiskit is like a set of sheet music and a conductor's baton—tools that help quantum composers (developers) create and refine their quantum algorithms. As Qiskit evolves, it will empower developers to push the boundaries of what's possible.

   - **Open Source and Community Growth:** The quantum community is like an orchestra, where each member contributes to the music. In the same way, the Qiskit community contributes to the growth of the platform, making it better for everyone.

Concepts Covered: Emerging Trends, Quantum Supremacy, Future of Qiskit

Now, let's break down these concepts into simple code examples, with explanations for each step.

---

1. Emerging Trends:

Quantum Machine Learning

Imagine you want to use quantum computing to help with machine learning tasks, like sorting notes in a symphony. Here's how you might start:

python

Code

```python
from qiskit import QuantumCircuit, Aer, execute
from qiskit.ml import QiskitMachineLearning


# Setting up a simple quantum circuit
qc = QuantumCircuit(2)
qc.h(0)  # Apply Hadamard gate to qubit 0, creating a superposition
qc.cx(0, 1)  # Apply CNOT gate, entangling qubits 0 and 1
qc.measure_all()  # Measure both qubits


# Simulating the circuit
backend = Aer.get_backend('qasm_simulator')
job = execute(qc, backend, shots=1024)
result = job.result()


# Quantum Machine Learning
# (This is just an example, QiskitMachineLearning would involve more
advanced setups)
qml = QiskitMachineLearning()
```

- **Hadamard Gate (h)**: Think of this as playing a note softly, creating a mix of sounds (superposition).

- **CNOT Gate (cx)**: This is like synchronizing two instruments, making them play in harmony (entanglement).

- **Measurement (measure_all)**: Recording the sound, so we know what we played (collapsing the quantum state to classical information).

Quantum Cryptography

This is like encrypting a musical score so only the right conductor can read it:

python

Code

```python
from qiskit import QuantumCircuit, execute, Aer
from qiskit.circuit.library import QFT

# Simple Quantum Fourier Transform Circuit (used in cryptography)
qc = QuantumCircuit(3)
qc.h([0, 1, 2])  # Apply Hadamard gates to all qubits
qc.append(QFT(3), [0, 1, 2])  # Apply Quantum Fourier Transform
qc.measure_all()  # Measure the qubits

# Simulating the circuit
backend = Aer.get_backend('qasm_simulator')
job = execute(qc, backend, shots=1024)
result = job.result()

# Output the result
print(result.get_counts())
```

- **Quantum Fourier Transform (QFT)**: Like translating the music into a secret code that only quantum musicians can read.

---

2. Quantum Supremacy

Let's say we want to demonstrate something only a quantum computer can do, like playing a musical piece too complex for classical instruments:

python

Code

```python
from qiskit import QuantumCircuit, Aer, execute
```

```python
# Create a circuit that demonstrates quantum supremacy
qc = QuantumCircuit(5)
qc.h([0, 1, 2, 3, 4])  # Apply Hadamard gates to create superposition
qc.measure_all()  # Measure all qubits

# Simulating the circuit
backend = Aer.get_backend('qasm_simulator')
job = execute(qc, backend, shots=1024)
result = job.result()

# Output the result
print(result.get_counts())
```

- **Superposition and Entanglement**: These allow quantum computers to explore many musical "paths" simultaneously, unlike classical computers, which can only follow one path at a time.

---

3. The Future of Qiskit

Qiskit will continue to evolve, just like a musical instrument gets better over time. New features will allow quantum composers to create even more complex and beautiful "music."

python

Code

```python
from qiskit import IBMQ, QuantumCircuit

# Loading IBMQ account
IBMQ.load_account()

# Create a simple circuit and run it on a real quantum computer
qc = QuantumCircuit(2)
```

```
qc.h(0)

qc.cx(0, 1)

qc.measure_all()


# Execute on a real device

provider = IBMQ.get_provider(hub='ibm-q')

backend = provider.get_backend('ibmq_quito')

job = execute(qc, backend, shots=1024)

result = job.result()


# Output the result

print(result.get_counts())
```

- **Real Quantum Hardware**: Like performing music live, running a quantum circuit on real hardware is the ultimate test of your quantum composition.

Summary

Each step in quantum computing is like composing a part of a symphony. You start with basic notes (qubits and gates), build up complexity (quantum algorithms), rehearse (simulate), and finally perform live (run on real quantum hardware). As we look to the future, quantum computing will evolve, much like how music evolves with new instruments and styles.

This journey of building quantum solutions with Qiskit is like being part of a quantum orchestra. Each developer contributes to the greater "music" of quantum computing, pushing the field forward and creating new possibilities for the future. Just like in music, the end is never really the end—there's always a new composition waiting to be written.

A dramatic and simpler summary of Qiskit. Each song will cover a concept from quantum computing and Qiskit, using analogies and poetic language.

Chapter 1: Introduction to Quantum Comaputing

Song 1: The Quantum Realm

Verse 1:

In the realm where qubits dance,

Superposition takes a chance.

A note of zero, a note of one,

Entangled together, they become one.

Verse 2:

Quantum states, a hidden song,

Playing melodies all day long.

Measurement ends the harmony,

Collapsing into certainty.

Verse 3:

Entanglement, a bond so tight,

Across the stars, through day and night.

Instant whispers, near or far,

A cosmic ballet, a quantum star.

Verse 4:

In this world, we find our start,

Quantum notes play from the heart.

A symphony of the unseen,

In the quantum realm, we dream.

Song 2: The Quantum Orchestra

Verse 1:

Imagine an orchestra, vast and grand,

Each qubit a musician in hand.

Superposition, their subtle art,

Creating music from the heart.

Verse 2:

Entangled duets, a perfect pair,

Harmonizing through the air.

Conducted by a hidden force,

A quantum conductor sets the course.

Verse 3:

Measurement, the final note,

Collapsing the wave, they wrote.

From all possibilities, one they choose,

In this symphony, they never lose.

Verse 4:

Qubits play their silent tune,

Underneath the quantum moon.

In their song, we find the key,

To unlock the quantum mystery.

Chapter 2: Setting Up the Quantum Stage

Song 3: Tuning the Instruments

Verse 1:

Before the symphony can start,

We must tune each qubit's part.

Install Qiskit, the first step,

Prepare the stage where they'll be kept.

Verse 2:

Sign up for IBM's cloud,

Where quantum notes are played out loud.

A quantum account, your ticket in,

To where the quantum tunes begin.

Verse 3:

Configure your toolkit, make it right,

For a performance that's pure delight.

Tuning instruments, setting the stage,

For the quantum notes to engage.

Verse 4:

With Qiskit installed, you're ready now,

To write quantum music, learn how.

A symphony awaits your hand,

In the quantum realm, you'll stand.

Chapter 3: The Quantum Conductor

Song 4: Designing the Circuit

Verse 1:

With baton in hand, the conductor starts,

Designing circuits, mapping parts.

Quantum gates, the notes they play,

Guiding qubits on their way.

Verse 2:

Hadamard gates, a gentle touch,

Superposition, means so much.

CNOT gates, entangle tight,

Creating harmony, day and night.

Verse 3:

Measure each qubit, capture the sound,

See where the quantum notes are bound.

In the circuit, music flows,

A quantum symphony, ever grows.

Verse 4:

The conductor's baton, precise and clear,

Directing qubits, far and near.

In this orchestration, we find our beat,

Quantum circuits, a rhythmic feat.

Chapter 4: The Symphony of Quantum Algorithms

Song 5: Quantum Algorithms

Verse 1:

Quantum algorithms, a grand design,

Solving problems, they redefine.

QFT and QPE, like notes in time,

Grover's search, a rhythmic rhyme.

Verse 2:

Variational methods, VQE,

Optimizing paths, in a quantum way.

QAOA, finding routes so clear,

In this symphony, algorithms steer.

Verse 3:

Composing pieces, intricate and bold,

Quantum algorithms, stories told.

Each note a solution, each chord a clue,

To mysteries old, and breakthroughs new.

Verse 4:

In this quantum composition, we find,

Algorithms that stretch the mind.

A masterpiece of logic and grace,

In the quantum symphony's embrace.

Chapter 5: Simulating the Quantum Symphony

Song 6: Dress Rehearsal

Verse 1:

Before the final performance takes its flight,

We simulate circuits, day and night.

Qiskit Aer, our rehearsal space,

Testing quantum notes in this place.

Verse 2:

Simulations, a practice run,

Ensuring the harmony, under the sun.

Errors noted, adjustments made,

For the quantum symphony's grand parade.

Verse 3:

Running circuits, checking the beat,

Ensuring the melody is sweet.

In this rehearsal, we perfect our art,

Before the live show, it must start.

Verse 4:

Simulation, the dress rehearsal's role,

Perfecting the performance, as a whole.

Preparing the symphony, for the stage,

In this quantum age, we engage.

Chapter 6: Performing on the Quantum Stage

Song 7: The Live Performance

Verse 1:

The stage is set, the lights are bright,

Running circuits, feels just right.

On real quantum hardware, we perform,

A symphony, breaking the norm.

Verse 2:

IBMQ, our stage so grand,

Executing quantum plans.

Each note precise, each gate in place,

In this performance, we find our grace.

Verse 3:

Live on hardware, the symphony sings,

Quantum notes, on ethereal strings.

A performance to remember, a moment so true,

In the quantum world, we pursue.

Verse 4:

With every qubit, the music flows,

On quantum hardware, it shows.

A live performance, a grand debut,

In the quantum realm, dreams come true.

Chapter 7: Interpreting the Quantum Melody

Song 8: Analyzing the Results

Verse 1:

When the performance ends, the audience claps,

Interpreting results, with careful maps.

Measurement outcomes, probability seen,

In the quantum melody, keen.

Verse 2:

Analyze the notes, understand the play,

What did the quantum music convey?

Error analysis, tuning the sound,

In the quantum results, insights are found.

Verse 3:

Probability distributions, a guide,

Showing where the quantum notes reside.

Each outcome, a piece of the song,

In the quantum melody, we belong.

Verse 4:

Interpreting results, reading the score,

Understanding the quantum encore.

In this analysis, we find our way,

To improve the symphony, day by day.

Chapter 8: Tuning the Quantum Orchestra

Song 9: Optimizing the Performance

Verse 1:

Fine-tuning instruments, refining the sound,

Optimizing circuits, where errors are found.

Circuit optimization, a delicate art,

Enhancing the music, from the start.

Verse 2:

Error mitigation, correcting the flow,

Ensuring the harmony, in the show.

Advanced techniques, to improve the play,

Making the quantum notes, stay.

Verse 3:

Optimization, the conductor's touch,

Refining the performance, means so much.

Each adjustment, a step towards grace,

In the quantum symphony's embrace.

Verse 4:

With tuning complete, the music shines,

A perfected symphony, in quantum lines.

Optimized and flawless, the final score,

In the quantum realm, forever more.

Chapter 9: The Quantum Encore

Song 10: Sharing the Symphony

Verse 1:

After the performance, an encore to share,

Deploying solutions, with utmost care.

Sharing with the community, the quantum art,

In this collaboration, we all take part.

Verse 2:

Open source contributions, a gift,

Helping the quantum community to lift.

Deploying solutions, for all to see,

In this quantum world, we are free.

Verse 3:

The curtain call, a final note,

Sharing the symphony, we wrote.

With each deployment, a story told,

In the quantum realm, bold.

Verse 4:

The encore, a celebration grand,

Sharing the music, hand in hand.

In the quantum community, we thrive,

Keeping the symphony alive.

Chapter 10: The Future of Quantum Symphony

Song 11: The Next Composition

Verse 1:

Looking ahead, the future's bright,

Quantum computing, reaching new heights.

Emerging trends, a path so clear,

In the quantum realm, we hold dear.

Verse 2:

Quantum supremacy, a goal we seek,

A peak performance, unique.

New compositions, waiting to be played,

In this quantum journey, we're not swayed.

Verse 3:

The future of Qiskit, evolving fast,

A toolkit for the ages, built to last.

With each update, new features bloom,

In the quantum symphony's room.

Verse 4:

As we look ahead, with hope and light,

The quantum future, shining bright.

A new symphony, yet to be known,

In the quantum realm, we have grown.

This collection of songs, each with its own unique melody and rhythm, paints the journey of quantum computing with Qiskit as a symphony. From understanding the basics to envisioning the future, each song captures a moment in the grand composition of quantum computing.